UPON THE MOUNTAINS

Upon The Mountains

Encouragement for your Journey

Donald L. Hood

Upon the Mountains
Encouragement for Your Journey

Published by Better Together Publishing
www.bettertogetherpublishing.com
ISBN-13: 9780692931257
ISBN-10: 0692931252

Scripture taken from King James Version
Public Domain
Updates to the language were made from the original languages.

FOREWORD

UPON THE MOUNTAIN is a look into the heart and mind of Don Hood, my father, who has not only been a dedicated father, husband, friend, pastor, and mentor but by all measurable respects, a true man of God. My hope is that you'll find encouragement, wisdom, and knowledge through each unique and heartfelt devotion. Words fail to express the depth of gratitude I have for Dad and his consistent example of what it means to be a Christian. Instead, I'll let the depth of the devotions to our Lord and Savior Jesus Christ allow you to get a glimpse of his steadfast faith.

For those who do not have a relationship with Jesus Christ, I pray this opens your eyes to your need of salvation...there is no greater need. To the believer, I pray you gain a better understanding of God's Word and become closer to him, serving him with everything you have.

I'm honored to be the youngest son of the greatest man that I've ever known,

In Humble Regards,
Reverend Jonathan P. Hood

INTRODUCTION

AFTER HAVING BEEN in gospel ministry for over forty years, I was impressed of the Holy Spirit to begin writing a weekly devotional. I felt that most of us Christians need a word of encouragement in our daily walks. It occurred to me that people will remember parts of the message they hear from the pulpit, but a written message can be available for generations to come. So, in 2014 I began to write. I sent this weekly devotional out to my congregation and others who wished to be included in the form of an email.

In 2016, my health began to decline. I knew something was not right, so I saw multiple doctors trying to figure out what was going on. Then, in May of 2017, doctors diagnosed me with a neuromuscular disease named amyotrophic lateral sclerosis (ALS), better known to some as Lou Gehrig's disease. This progressive disease affects muscle function and worsens over time.

It has been amazing to see God's plan for my last days unfolding before me even in the midst of the struggles. While I still pastor a small church in the mountains of North Georgia, I realize that my time in the pulpit will soon end. It is a great source of encouragement to know that God can continue to use me through the devotionals He compelled me to begin long before my ALS diagnosis.

I am so blessed to have a loving wife and to be the father of two loving sons and a daughter. Both my sons are pastors, and my daughter works in the healthcare field. Unbeknownst to me, my oldest son, Chad, had been saving the devotionals I wrote. He encouraged me to continue writing, and so I did. Then I was encouraged to have the devotionals published. Chad has worked on the editing and publishing of this book, and without his help, I could not have completed it.

It is my prayer that this devotional will be a source of encouragement for all who read it for years to come.

Donald Lee Hood

THIRSTY

---

*But whosoever drinks of the water that I shall give
him shall never thirst.*
John 4:14

READ JOHN 4:1–26.

J ESUS HAD TO pass through Samaria, and he came to a town of
Samaria called Sychar. A certain woman was there who had a
need in her life only Jesus could satisfy.

> *Now Jacob's well was there. Jesus, therefore, being
> wearied with his journey, sat on the well: and it
> was about noon. There came a woman of Samaria
> to draw water: Jesus said to her, "Give me drink."*

—JOHN 4:6–7

Jesus had made a special trip to Jacob's well for the purpose of meeting this woman. Was she someone unique? Most certainly! And this lady was a sinner in need of a savior. She was likely alone because other women of the town had no desire to be seen with her. It was customary for the women to come together to draw water for the needs of the day, yet this woman was alone. The text tells us she had been married five times and was living in an ungodly relationship at the time Jesus met her. Jesus didn't introduce himself to her because she was good; he introduced himself to her because HE IS GOOD.

Jesus said to her, "Give me drink." While he was thirsting for natural water, he knew she was thirsty in a very different way. She was thirsting for spiritual water that brings life. She had been carrying her water pot to Jacob's well each day only to need it refilled the next day. How many people are lugging around the same old water pots of guilt, shame, fear, and worry, day after day? They may be coming to a well of religion, but somehow, they are never quite satisfied. They go to church week after week, hearing about Jesus and singing along with the others, but still carrying the same old water pot and remaining spiritually thirsty.

Jesus said to her—as he says to a dying and thirsty world— "Whosoever drinks of the water that I shall give him shall never thirst; but the water that I shall give him shall be in him a well of water springing up into everlasting life" (John 4:14). The relationship we have with God through Jesus is a personal one. When we come to know him as personal savior, there may be many people around us, but our experience of saving grace is a very intimate. Many know about Jesus, but knowing about him is not enough.

Having knowledge about him is good, but it will not save us from our sins. Jesus said, "You must be born again" (John 3:7).

After coming to know Jesus personally, the woman left her water pot, went into the city, and told everyone, "Come, see a man that told me all the things that ever I did: Is this not the Christ?" (John 4:28). Once you've met the Savior, there is no keeping it to yourself. You will want to tell others what he has done for you.

To this day, Jesus invites everyone to come and drink freely of the water of life. Lay down the burdensome water pots of guilt, fear, and shame, and rejoice in the liberty of God's amazing grace.

- What are some of the wells you have gone to in hopes of quenching your spiritual thirsts? Do they ever satisfy in the end?
- Today, seek to turn to Jesus moment by moment, and allow him to satisfy you.
- Are you spiritually thirsty? Go to Jesus and express your need to him.

NEVERTHELESS

And Simon (Peter) answering said unto him,
Master, we have toiled all the night, and have
taken nothing:
Nevertheless at your word I will let down the net.
Luke 5:5

READ LUKE 5:1–15.

BEFORE BECOMING FULL-TIME disciples of Jesus, Peter, James, and John were fishermen by trade. They knew the fishing business. They knew the Sea of Galilee. They knew where the fish were and where they were not. They also knew that the time for fishing was at night, not during the heat of the day. No professional fishermen would ever attempt to fish at the time Jesus directed Simon to let down his nets. And yet the disciples had fished the whole night before and caught nothing.

Jesus entered one of the ships and requested Simon Peter to thrust out a little from the shore. Jesus then taught the people from his spot on the boat, knowing that sound travels much better across open water. When he had finished the lesson, he told Peter, "Launch out into the deep, and let down your nets for a catch" (Luke 5:4). The teaching wasn't over.

Can you imagine what must have been going through Peter's mind at that moment? "What? Let down our nets? That makes no sense. This Jesus is certainly a good teacher, but he obviously knows nothing about fishing." I suspect he remembered how Jesus healed his wife's mother and so many others as he responded, "Master, we have toiled all the night, and have taken nothing: NEVERTHELESS at your word" (Luke 5:5, emphasis added).

Against all that made sense to Peter, he said, "Nevertheless." "Faith is the substance of things hoped for, the evidence of things not seen" (Hebrews 11:1). If we are to experience great catches in life, there will be times when we must say, "Nevertheless, at your word, Lord, I will let down my net." Up to that moment, the disciples' primary purpose was to live for themselves. But all that changed when Peter had his nevertheless moment. After that, it became all about Jesus. Verse 11 tells us, "They forsook all, and followed him."

Isn't it comforting to know that God is in complete control, even when you've toiled all night, done all you can, and there is nothing else to do but wash your nets? In those times, he knows and cares. You may be in a time of discouragement right now. The bills are due, you need groceries, and you just need a big catch. Remember that we have a savior who has not—nor will ever—left us or forsaken us. Instead, he says, "Launch out into the deep." Examine where you are spiritually, emotionally, and maybe even financially. Be willing to move in faith. Then hear and obey his Word. Peter changed his location and received the blessing through his obedience.

Jesus said, "Follow me, and I will make you fishers of men" (Matthew 4:19). May we all say, "Nevertheless, Lord, I will follow you!"

- What is keeping you from saying, "Nevertheless"? Turn to God in faith and begin an incredible journey as you follow the Lord.
- Are there areas of your life in which you are not walking by faith?
- What would it look like for you to walk in faith in some of those areas? Write them down and get a clear picture of what your life could be.

SEASONS

*To every thing there is a season, and a time to
every purpose under the heaven.*
Ecclesiastes 3:1

READ ECCLESIASTES 3:1–11.

FALL IS SUCH a beautiful time of year. The air is crisp and cooler, the trees are changing color, and the days are getting shorter. One of my favorite things is the smell of hardwood smoke coming from a fireplace on a frosty fall morning. As time brings about the changing seasons on earth, it also brings about the changing seasons of our lives. In the springtime, we play as children before we move into the summer of our adulthood. During those summer days, we may be busy raising our children, building our careers, and making a living. But summer always leads to the fall, when we begin to feel the change that time has brought about in these mortal bodies. The years of work have paid off, and we see the hope of grandchildren and of enjoying the rewards of life.

The good news is that, whatever season we may find ourselves in today, God has a plan and purpose for us. Many Christians have the attitude that because they don't have the energy and vigor of their younger years, they can sit on the sidelines and let others carry on with the Lord's work. The truth is that God is not finished with you yet. If your work were completed here, he would have already carried you home.

With the hand of God upon him, Moses did his greatest work for God during the autumn and winter of his life. A wise man once said, "God is not nearly as interested in our ability as he is in our availability." Many of the challenges that face our communities, our nations, and our churches call for the experience and wisdom of those who are in the autumn of life. Rather than sit by and talk about how we would do this or that differently, maybe we need to seek God's guidance, get off the bench, and get in the game!

Perhaps you are in a season of change. Know this: God is preparing you and equipping you for good works that he prepared beforehand and desires you to walk in (Ephesians 2:10). Whether you are young or old, the lesson is the same. Yield and be available to be used where the Lord places you. Wherever you are, be all there, and hold on! God will use you.

No matter the season, God has a purpose and plan in it. God is not finished with us yet, so let's get busy for the King's sake and enjoy the season.

- Is God calling you to some place of service in the kingdom? If so, let him have his way, knowing that he is always leading us toward life, fullness, and ultimate victory.
- Ask God to give you clarity about how he would like to use you in the season of life in which you find yourself.
- Enjoy this season of your life. Let a heart of thankfulness guide you as you spend time praising God. Remember, young ones are always looking for the next season, while the older are wishing to go back. Live every day so that when you look back, you can do so with joy.

STRENGTH FOR THE DAY

And he said unto me, My grace is sufficient for
you:
for my strength is made perfect in weakness.
2 Corinthians 12:9

READ 2 CORINTHIANS 12:7–10.

WE CONSIDER THE life of the apostle Paul to be a great example of what the authentic Christian life should be. Yet Paul was very swift to connect any virtues in his life to Christ. Meekness, humility, and faith in the life of the believer cultivate the soil from which the flowers of God's glory grow and flourish.

But God has chosen the foolish things of the world
to confound the wise; and God has chosen the weak

things of the world to confound the things which
are mighty; And low things of the world, and
things which are despised, has God chosen, yes, and
things which are not, to bring to nothing things
that are: That no flesh should glory in his presence.

—1 CORINTHIANS 1:27–29

The world sees its own bright flowers and thinks that they are the rare and exalted things. And in the world's eyes, such thoughts might be correct. However, the flowers' shallow roots and quickly fading colors will not stand the tests of time or eternity.

It is not the most talented, the best educated, or the most gifted who blooms the brightest in God's garden. Rather, it is the weak, sickly, fading flower—the one that requires the nurturing and direct attention of the heavenly gardener—that will bloom brightest. The bloom that has been watered by the Word, fertilized in God's grace, and exposed to the direct sunlight of God's Son is the bloom that endures and flowers into rare beauty. The flowers of the garden that are left to fend for themselves through pride, self-worth, and worldliness will soon fade. To those who truly desire to glorify the Father, he will give divine strength for every need.

So be of good courage, Christian. Are you feeling weak today? God is preparing you to receive strength. Are you feeling worthless and insignificant? God is about to bring about a blooming in your life that will bless others and glorify him. Remember, "When I am weak then am I strong" (2 Corinthians 12:10).

- Are there hardships or situations that are heavy on your heart? If so, write them down.
- What does God want you to do with those things? (Philippians 4:6)
- You do not have to deal with life on your own. Turn to the Lord in prayer and give whatever is heavy on your heart to him. Ask him to go before you, prepare the way, and walk with you as you deal with people, situations, and circumstances.

CONSISTENT AND AUTHENTIC

For to set the mind on the flesh is death;
but to be spiritually minded is life and peace.
Romans 8:6

READ ROMANS 8:1–8.

WHILE WE AS believers must live in this world, the Bible tells us we are "not of the world" (John 17:16). The Apostle Paul instructs us in Romans 12:2, "Be not conformed to this world: but be transformed by the renewing of your mind." We often have the choice of what influences our thinking. We can choose the type of music to which we listen as well as the kinds of entertainment we watch. All these things have an impact on our spiritual lives.

Question: What do you set your mind on during the week? Is it set on seeking the Lord, or is it seeking the ways of the world and the will of your fallen flesh? You can't be spiritually minded if you continually inundate your mind and heart with music that dishonors God but then try to sing "Oh, How I Love Jesus" on the weekend. We need to be careful of what we allow to influence our lives and our families.

The world is looking for something different, something authentic. Unfortunately, what they are seeing in the lives of many believers—or those who claim to be—does not match up. The hypocrisy is easy to see from the world's perspective.

Let us we examine our lives in the light of God's Word. If repentance is needed, may we repent, praying that God gives us a singleness of mind and heart and a love for Jesus that is unmistakable. That is what the world needs.

- Are there areas of your life in which you sense God revealing some type of hypocrisy?
- If so, take them to God in humility and ask him for the strength to turn those things over to him.
- If God is pointing out some things that need to be cleaned up, do not resist. He is leading you to life, peace, and joy that only comes through a relationship with him. Spend time opening your heart up to the Lord.

SWEET ENCOURAGEMENT

Then Jonathan said, My father has troubled
the land: see, I pray you, how my eyes have been
brightened, because I tasted a little of this honey."
1 Samuel 14:29

READ PROVERBS 16:24.

S WEET TO THE taste and nourishing to the body is honey.
Likewise, sweet to the spirit and nourishing to the soul is the
sweetness of the gospel message—the good news that Jesus came
and died on the cross to take the penalty we incurred through our
sin. Because the penalty of sin was death, he died for us, and he
now offers us his life.

Having tasted the sweetness of God's amazing grace through
the message of the gospel, our eyes are now open to the truth. Jesus
said, "I am the way, the truth, and the life: no man comes unto

the Father, but by me" (John 14:6). Romans 5:1 says, "Therefore being justified by faith, we have peace with God through our Lord Jesus Christ." The peace of God is to the soul like honey is to the tongue; they are both sweet and nourishing.

Jonathan was strengthened and encouraged by the honey he ate that day. It brought renewed life to him. The world likewise is in desperate need of a renewed life, and we should be sharing the rich message of God's mercy and grace with this lost and dying world. Jonathan's eyes were opened to the truth with just a taste of honey, just as the Word of God opens our eyes to behold the goodness and glory of God.

As children of God who have already tasted the honey of the gospel, may our appetite for the Word of God be strong and our vision for truth be sharp. There is no substitute for honey. There may be other sweeteners, but there is nothing like the real thing. There is also no substitute for the gospel message. The world may offer cheap imitations, but only the gospel can give lasting satisfaction. Only the Word of God can give light to those in darkness and satisfy the hungry soul.

- Have you understood and received the good news that Jesus died for your sins? Now he offers forgiveness, life, and—most importantly—a relationship with him. If you have not yet done so, take time now to receive him and his forgiveness. Ask him to forgive you as you open your heart to him.
- Are you looking for hope and help somewhere other than the pure honey of God's Word? If so, confess that and

turn to the Lord for help. Commit to spending time in the Bible daily.

- Do you know someone who is going in the wrong direction? Is someone in your life looking for peace and fulfillment in things of this world—things that can never satisfy? Pray for those people and ask God for the opportunity to speak to them in love, truth, and grace.

THE SHEPHERD'S VOICE

My sheep hear my voice, and I know them, and
they follow me: And I give unto them eternal life;
and they shall never perish, neither shall any man
pluck them out of my hand. My Father, which
gave them to me, is greater than all; and no man is
able to pluck them out my Father's hand. I and my
Father are one.
John 10:27–30

READ JOHN 10:1–30.

ONLY THOSE WHO have heard Jesus speak can say, "Never has a man spoken like this man" (John 7:46). Just as sheep know the voice of their shepherd, we that are his have heard and know his voice. No one but Jesus could ever say, "I lay down my life, that I might take it again. No man takes it from me, but I lay it down of myself. I have power to lay it down, and I have the power to take it again"(John 10:17–18).

> *And he said unto them, Why are you fearful, O you of little faith? Then he arose, and rebuked the winds and the sea; and there was a great calm. But the men marveled, saying, What manner of man is this, that even the winds and the sea obey him!*

—MATTHEW 8:26–27

When your soul is being tossed about on the sea of condemnation, storm clouds of guilt and shame are all around, and fear grips your heart, you can cry out, "Lord, save me." Do you hear the same voice his disciples heard saying, "Peace; be still"? Of all the familiar voices you know, which one has the authority to say, "Come unto me, all you that labor and are heavy laden, and I will give you rest" (Matthew 11:28)? The answer, of course, is none but Jesus. The reason no man has ever spoken like this man is because Jesus was no ordinary man; he was God in the flesh. Who else could say, "Let not your heart be troubled: you believe in God, believe also in me. In my Father's house are many mansions: if it were not so, I would have told you. I go to prepare a place for you. And if I go and prepare a place for you, I will come again, and receive you unto myself; that where I am, there you may be also" (John 14:1-3)?

This same Jesus is still speaking today to all who will listen. He still speaks with the same power and authority he spoke with when he walked among men. He still gives instruction, confidence, peace, joy, and comfort to all who will hear. He is still the "bread of life" to the hungry soul (John 6:35) and the water of life to the soul that is athirst (John 4:14). He is still a friend to the lonely, hope to the discouraged, and strength to the weak. He still speaks, and the blind are made to see. He still speaks, and the deaf hear. He still speaks, and the sick are made whole. His voice is still louder than the thunder yet gentler than the dove. He still speaks to the poorest of the poor and awakens kings on their beds in the middle of the night. The question is not "Does he still speak?" The question is "Are you listening?"

- Be encouraged today. God is speaking through his Word and by the power of the Holy Spirit. Spend time being quiet before the Lord. Ask the Lord to help you hear and understand what he is saying to you.
- When he speaks, receive what he is saying in faith, knowing that he is always seeking to draw you near and guide you on your journey.
- Spend time being quiet before the Lord. Meditate upon his Word and listen to his voice.

HIS STRENGTH

And Jehoshaphat feared, and set himself to seek the
LORD,
and proclaimed a fast throughout all Judah.
2 Chronicles 20:3

READ 2 CHRONICLES 20:1–30.

To KING JEHOSHAPHAT, it appeared that the odds were overwhelming. The people of Judah were about to be overrun
and destroyed. It seems to me that Jehoshaphat had three possible
choices in this dilemma. Come to think about, you and I are
also faced with these same options when our adversary the devil
comes against us, as he surely will.

First, Jehoshaphat could have just surrendered. Surrender
appears to be the choice many make today as they wave the white
flag of compromise. If you make this choice, fear, doubt, and

worry will soon occupy the promised land of your soul. The ground that once brought forth the fruit of the spirit will begin to yield the weeds and ways of the world.

Second, Jehoshaphat could have chosen to prepare himself in the battle garment of pride. He could have taken an arrogant attitude saying, "I am the king, and I can handle any enemy that comes my way." We can look around and see casualties of battles from some who have decided to rely upon their own strength and power. It is amazing to see how often we can face a situation and try to handle it in our own strength. In those times, we often deceive ourselves. Many kings have vainly trusted in their own power, and so have many of us.

Thankfully, Jehoshaphat chose the third option. He confessed his fear and admitted that he was in a helpless situation without the mighty hand of God. He said, "We do not know what to do" (2 Chronicles 20:12). In times of uncertainty, it can be difficult to admit, "We just do not know," but we should never fear to come to that point. After all, it is a place of truth and a place of realization. In those moments of honesty and clarity, we realize that we are weak and need help. As God told the Apostle Paul, "My grace is sufficient for you: for my strength is made perfect in weakness" (2 Corinthians 12:9). That is the place to which Jehoshaphat came, and it led God's people to seek the Lord.

No matter how smart we are, no matter how strong we feel, there are times and battles that come when the only thing we can do is go to God and confess that we just don't have the answers. It is precisely in those times we are met with the power, presence, and wisdom of God.

- What are some fears that you have in life? Where do you need God to move on your behalf?
- It is amazing how often we want to handle life in our power, strength, and wisdom. God is waiting for you to come to him with your needs. Write down your concerns and begin to bring them to God every day. Be specific.
- Yield to the Lord today. In a state of humility, bring everything that is on your heart to him in thankfulness. He is a Father who will not ignore his children.

THE GOOD SHEPHERD

*He makes me to lie down in green pastures: he
leads me beside the still waters. He restores my
soul: he leads me in the paths of righteousness for
his name's sake.*
Psalm 23:2–3

READ PSALM 23.

THE LOVE OF our Lord is like that of a loving shepherd for his
sheep. The most familiar Psalm is most likely Psalm 23. The
psalmist explains how God is like a shepherd in how he leads us.
In the New Testament, the idea of the shepherd becomes beauti-
fully clear in John 10:14 where Jesus said, "I am the good shepherd, and know my sheep, and my sheep know me."

The love of the shepherd for his flock is boundless. Not
only does he make provision for his entire flock, but he cares

particularly for each one of his sheep. He also gives protection to his flock. "Yes, though I walk through the valley of the shadow of death, I will fear no evil: for you are with me; your rod and your staff they comfort me" (Psalm 23:4). What a beautiful picture of God's love for us. He is very intentional in his care for us. He knows where to lead us, and he knows how to protect us. To be in his flock is very special. Sadly, not everyone is a part of his flock.

All of us are like sheep in this way: before we were part of his flock, we were all wandering away. We were lost sheep in a cruel world. Isaiah 53:6 states, "All we like sheep have gone astray; we have turned every one to his own way; and the LORD has laid on him the iniquity of us all." Wandering and lonely sheep are always in danger, and before we knew the Lord, we were in danger as well.

Each one of us was born with a fallen nature that leads us to sin. The bad news about sinning against a holy, just, and eternal God is that we cannot just sin and rebel without consequences. If that were a possibility, he could not be a just God. Thankfully, in addition to being just, he is also merciful. We were going to pay the penalty for our sins. That penalty is eternal separation from God—everlasting death. But God in his mercy sent his son, Jesus, to pay the penalty for our sin.

Jesus took our sins upon himself on the cross. Now the penalty for sin has been paid. Since the punishment is paid, he offers life to those who come to him in faith! At the moment we accept his offer of life and forgiveness, he becomes a shepherd to us, and we are a part of his flock, the church. He is truly the good shepherd.

- Are you a part of God's flock? If not, turn to him in faith, asking him to forgive you and make you his.
- If you are a believer and following the Lord, spend time thanking the Lord for his goodness and love. Take a few minutes to contemplate these truths deeply.
- Do you know people who need the love of the Good Shepherd? Spend time praying for them. Ask God to give you opportunities to show them the love of God and his wondrous salvation.

JOY IN THE MORNING

For his anger endures but a moment; in his favor
is life:
weeping may endure for a night, but joy comes in the morning.
Psalm 30:5

READ I CORINTHIANS 15:35–49.

How comforting to the believer to know that God saves the best for last! Just as it was on the first day, when God's creative work began with darkness and ended with the glorious light of morning, so shall the last day be. Darkness was upon the face of the deep, but God said, "Let there be light: and there was light" (Genesis 1:3). It may be that you are going through a dark season of trials and tribulation. Sometimes when we are in the midst of struggles, the darkness seems overwhelming, but be of good cheer: "Weeping may endure for a night, but joy comes in the morning" (Psalm 30:5). No matter how thick the darkness may seem, let us rejoice in knowing that morning is soon to come.

Before the deliverance of the children of Israel, there came the darkness of bondage. Before reaching the Promised Land, the Israelites came to the wilderness. Before the harvest comes the sowing. Before the victory comes the battle. Before glory comes tribulation. Before the resurrection came the crucifixion. Before we receive our new glorified bodies, we must shed the old.

While it seems the forces of darkness and of this world surround us on every side, do not fear. God is in complete control, and the glorious morning that will never end is soon to come. While we are still here in this body of death, let us rejoice in knowing that God is saving the best for last.

- All men have trials and trouble in this life. But how does God use them in life of the believer? (First Peter 1:6-9)
- Why is it so important not to focus on the difficulties but instead look to Jesus as our hope?
- How does knowing that God never leaves nor forsakes help you in day-to-day struggles and offer long-term hope for your life?

Make Your Stand

Put on the whole armor of God,
that you may be able to stand against the wiles of
the devil.
Ephesians 6:11

Read Ephesians 6:10–18.

As heirs and joint heirs with Christ, we are not frail, weak peasants at the mercy of this world. Paul says, "No, in all these things we are more than conquerors through him that loved us" (Romans 8:37). All too often, however, we seem to be overwhelmed by the enemy's assault. Our enemy is crafty and cunning. He knows that a weakened adversary is more easily defeated. Rather than mounting an all-out assault on a well-equipped, well-trained warrior, he will do his best to weaken the child of God and then attack from all sides. He sends his spies of complacency, selfishness, apathy, and ignorance of the Word throughout the camp of the Christian mind and heart. Once he has a weakened his enemy through these means, he can mount the assault.

This why Paul in his letter to the Ephesians instructed them to "put on the whole armor of God" (Ephesians 6:11). He admonished them to "stand therefore, having your loins girded about with truth, and having on the breastplate of righteousness; And your feet shod with the preparation of the gospel of peace; Above all, taking the shield of faith, with which you shall be able to quench all the fiery darts of the wicked. And take the helmet of salvation, and the sword of the Spirit, which is the word of God" (Ephesians 6:14–17). Notice that the only offensive weapon Paul describes is the sword of the Spirit. The sword of the Spirit is not a feeling or an experience; it is the Word of God. If a soldier is unfamiliar with his weapons, it doesn't matter how well equipped he is, he will not be able to wield the weapon effectively.

Do you think that the creator of the universe—who describes himself as EL ELYON (God Most High), El OLAM (The Everlasting God), and EL SHADDAI (Lord God Almighty)—intends for his children to go around with a defeated attitude? I think not! "For the weapons of our warfare are not carnal, but mighty through God to the pulling down of strong holds" (2 Corinthians 10:4). Believer, is there a stronghold in your life? Maybe you are held captive by worry, fear, doubt, or a sin that God keeps bringing up but that you have not dealt with. If so, confess, repent, and begin to equip yourself with the weapons of our warfare. Pray, get in the Word, study your Bible, and fellowship with other believers.

Jesus won the victory over death and hell at Calvary, and he wants his children to walk victoriously and joyfully in this world. Why not begin today?

- Do you sense spiritual warfare in your life or in your family? If so, how do you fight that battle according to the Scripture above?
- Take your concerns and difficulties to God in prayer. Read his Word that you might be strengthened and prepared.
- Never begin a morning without spending time with God in preparation for your day. Make a commitment to devoting the beginning of your day to him.

THANKFUL

And one of them, when he saw that he was healed,
turned back, and with a loud voice glorified God,
And fell down on his face at his feet, giving him
thanks:
and he was a Samaritan.
Luke 17:15–16

READ LUKE 17:11–19.

THE MEN IN Luke 17: 11–19 all had some things in common: they were all lepers who needed and wanted healing, they all cried out to Jesus, and they acknowledged him as "Master," asking for mercy.

Leprosy in Scripture was considered unclean and a sign of sin (Leviticus 13–14). It separated the leper from fellowship with the congregation, just as sin separates us from fellowship with God and other believers. The focus in Luke 17:11–19, however, is on thanksgiving. Jesus said to all ten, "Go show yourselves unto the priests. And it came to pass that, as they went, they were cleansed" (Luke 17:14). They were all recipients of a great miracle, but not all of them had an attitude of thankfulness.

Are we any different? Are we like the one who returned and fell at Jesus' feet in thanksgiving? Or are we like the other nine men? Do we want the gift, or do we want the giver? Do we want the healing, or do we want the healer? How many times have we cried out to God in the midst of a storm only to continue on our course after the storm has passed? True thanksgiving is more than just bowing our heads and saying, "Thank you, Lord, for this bountiful meal we are about to eat." It is an attitude of gratitude displayed in our daily lives.

Thanksgiving must involve both thanks and giving. Thankfulness is an attitude; giving is an action. It seems we take so much for granted these days. The prayer life of many would read more like a menu of our daily wants than a prayer of thanksgiving. Do we tell people how blessed we are to have them as a part of our lives? Or do we just assume they know?

May we not be like the nine who went their way without stopping to give thanks but rather like the one who loved the giver, not just the gift. I am thankful for you, dear reader. I pray that God will bless you and draw you to himself in these days.

- Think of all the ways God has blessed you. Give thanks to the Lord as you think them.
- Consider the giver of all blessings. Turn your heart to him and direct your thanksgiving toward him and not just what he gives.
- Be thankful today. Tell others that you are thankful for them. Recognize the giving of others and develop the attitude of gratitude.

ENCOURAGE ONE ANOTHER

*Love not the world, neither the things that are in
the world.
If any man love the world, the love of the Father is
not in him.
1 John 2:15*

READ 1 JOHN 2:15–17.

W HILE "STRAIT IS the gate, and narrow is the way" that leads
to eternal life (Matthew 7:14), the way is wide enough for
Christian brothers and sisters to walk alongside each other as we
journey toward the wonderful land of promise. Fellowship with
Christ and other believers is to the Christian what life-giving water
is to a rose. Though we are in the world, we are not of the world.

The Scriptures give a distinct contrast between the walk of
the Christian and the walk of those who have no relationship

with Christ. One of the distinguishing trademarks is our fellowship with each other. The fellowship of believers is a source of strength. It comes from having a common transformational relationship with God through his son Jesus Christ. While we may come from many different walks of life, different backgrounds, and even different cultures, there is something that we have in common. It is the blood of Jesus, the Lamb of God who takes away the sin of the world. This transformational common thread transcends customs, cultures, and languages. It did so on the day of Pentecost, and still does today.

That which we have seen and heard declare we
unto you, that you also may have fellowship with
us: and truly our fellowship is with the Father, and
with his Son Jesus Christ. And these things write
we unto you, that your joy may be full.

—1 JOHN 1:3–4

First and foremost, we need fellowship with the Lord, but we also need the fellowship of other believers. Simply put, we need each other. We are all a part of the same body: the body of Christ. As such, it should be the desire of us all to help strengthen one another. Our fellowship gives strength to the weak, faith to the fearful, joy to the downhearted, peace to the troubled. It exalts us when we're humble, humbles us when we're prideful, and corrects us when we are wrong.

Do you want to have a meaningful and purpose-filled day? Try encouraging another believer who is going through a tough time. The fellowship that you share today may make an astounding difference in someone's life. You are where you are today for a purpose. So often, we are so distracted by our own problems that we forget about everybody else. A short time of fellowship or a kind word of encouragement might make all the difference in the world to someone. So go ahead, make somebody's day. Spend time with the Lord and then with other believers. You'll be glad you did.

- The strongest encouragement you will ever receive comes from spending time with the Lord. Spend time praying and having a conversation with him.
- Encourage someone today. Use social media, a text, a phone call, or conversation as a tool to encourage individuals who need it.
- Make spending time with other believers a priority. Get involved with a local church that teaches the Bible. Don't just be a consumer; seek to give and to use your talents and spiritual gifts for the encouragement of others as well.

THE POWER OF PRAISE

*And at midnight Paul and Silas prayed, and sang
praises unto God: and the prisoners heard them.
And suddenly there was a great earthquake, so that
the foundations of the prison were shaken: and
immediately all the doors were opened, and every
one's bands were loosed.*
Acts 16:25–26

READ ACTS 16:16–31 AND PSALM 150.

I MAGINE BEING BEATEN, cast into a filthy Roman prison, and
chained up. Your only offense is casting a demon out of a young
woman who was in desperate need. In such a time, it would be
easy to question God and complain about how unfair this whole
deal is. While that may be many of our responses to persecution,
it was not the reaction of Paul and Silas. Rather than look at their

circumstances, they decided to turn their attention to the goodness of God.

Many of us are impeded by what I call "situational prayer and praise." We petition God for his help when we are in trouble, and our praise comes after he delivers us. You should certainly bring your burdens and cares to him, "casting all your care upon him; for he cares for you" (1 Peter 5:7). But what if we do as Paul and Silas did in that difficult time and simply praise God for who he is and his magnificent work? Could our praise change the way we see our circumstances? It absolutely could. When we praise God, our hearts are redirected. They are tuned in to what the Spirit of God is doing, and we are encouraged in our faith.

In Psalm 150, we are instructed to "praise the Lord" no less than thirteen times. Nowhere are we told to glorify God only when we feel like it. On the contrary, we are to praise him at all times for his mighty acts and excellent greatness. And we are to do so with the trumpet, stringed instruments, pipes, and crashing cymbals! The time or the situation does not matter; his praise is to be on our lips in times of great happiness as well as in the darkness of persecution.

As Paul and Silas sat there giving glory to the Lord, something unbelievable happened. There was an earthquake! God began to shake things up and shake things loose. Prisoners who were asleep no doubt began to wake up. Doors began to open, shackles began to fall off, and the prisoners were set free.

God has not changed nor has his power diminished. If we as his children will continue in prayer and praise, we too will see locked doors open, the chains of sin loosed, and prisoners set free. So when you don't feel like praying, pray anyway! When you don't feel like praising God, praise him anyway!

- "Praise him for his mighty acts: praise him according to his excellent greatness" (Psalm 150:2).
- Spend time praising God. Glorify him for who he is and then for the great things he has done.
- Spend time being specific in your praise as you worship God for who he has been to you and the gracious blessings he has given you.

Stop and Listen

You are distracted and troubled about many
things:
But one thing is needful.
Luke 10:41–42

Read Luke 10:38–42.

W HAT A WONDERFUL hostess we find in Martha, the sister
of Mary and Lazarus. Jesus had entered the village where
the sisters lived, and Martha invited him in. She had the heart
of a faithful servant, and it was her desire to wait upon the Lord.
But something was not right. Her heart seemed to be out of bal-
ance, and her priorities had become confused. We know for sure
that Martha was distracted and was running around trying to get
everything finished, and Jesus noticed it.

Mary, on the other hand, sat at Jesus' feet and listened to him
talk. Martha, seeing her sister sitting at the master's feet, became

frustrated. Perhaps she had thoughts like, "It's not fair. It's just not right. I'm doing all the work, and there she sits, doing nothing but listening." We have all had those moments when we feel like we are the ones sacrificing while everyone else enjoys life. We are the ones doing the work, and others are reaping the rewards. Martha was possibly struggling with that kind of thinking. Finally, she had enough and said to Jesus, "Lord, do you not care that my sister has left me to serve alone? Tell her therefore to help me" (Luke 10:40). The joy of serving the Lord with gladness had been replaced with an attitude of envy and self-pity. Martha's focus had shifted from Jesus to herself and what she saw as her self-serving sister.

Jesus, knowing Martha's heart, said, "Martha, Martha, you are distracted and troubled about many things: But one thing is needful: and Mary has chosen that good part, which shall not be taken away from her" (Luke 10:41–42). We see in this picture that those who walk closely with our Lord can become so busy helping that we stop hearing—so busy trying that we stop trusting. Martha had become so troubled and full of care that she had completely lost the joy and peace of just being in the presence of Jesus.

Over the years, I have seen many pastors and hard working lay people in the church become so frustrated. They feel alone in service the Lord. When this happens, it is easy to begin to focus on how hard we are trying and how little others seem to be doing. These are times when we need just to stop, sit down, and listen to the sweet, tender voice of our master.

Of course, we serve the Lord by serving one another. But let us not get so busy serving in our power that we forget to listen and wait upon the Lord. He has something to say to you today if you will only stop and listen.

- What is distracting you from listening to the Lord? What are those tasks, worries, or responsibilities that you have allowed to be more important than your time with God?
- What other things crowd your time and keep you from spending time listening to the Lord?
- Dwight L. Moody said, "We ought to see the face of God every morning before we see the face of man." Make meeting with the Lord a priority. Begin your day in his presence.

GOD WHO IS NEAR

Am I a God who is near, says the LORD, and not
a God far off?
Can any hide himself in secret places that I shall
not see him? says the LORD.
Do not I fill heaven and earth? says the LORD.
Jeremiah 23:23–24

READ PHILIPPIANS 4:10–13.

WHEN THE SKY is blue and the warm winds of prosperity, good health, and happiness blow gently upon our backs, it's easy to sing praises to the King. We have no problem quoting Paul's passage to the church at Philippi: "I can do all things through Christ which strengthens me" (Philippians 4:13). We easily repeat Romans 8:37: "We are more than conquerors through him that loved us." When the road of life ahead is straight and seems to be free of bumps and potholes, we think we can handle all the darts of discouragement the enemy can hurl. But when the darts actually come—and they will—how will we fair? If we only focus on the successes and feel good stories, how will we respond when troubles come? We may find ourselves asking the questions, "What is wrong with me? What did I do to deserve this?"

It is encouraging to read the biblical examples of people like us who had great difficulties dealing with despair and hard times. The man Job was sorry for the day he was born. He said, "Let the day perish wherein I was born" (Job 3:3). Even with all of his wealth and wisdom, Solomon said, "I hated life; because the work that is done under the sun is grievous unto me" (Ecclesiastes 2:17). Elijah requested that God would allow him to die (1 Kings 19:4). Jonah said, "Therefore now, O LORD, take, I beg you, my life from me; for it is better for me to die than to live" (Jonah 4:3). Talk about down and out! These guys were depressed, and their laments are nearly too hard to read.

All of these men had one thing in common besides being broken. What they had was a relationship with God. When they reached the very bottom, they were at the end of themselves. It was in those moments that the precious presence of God became apparent, and God communed with them. God does not ever shy away from the human experience, nor does he excuse it. He allows us to come to these broken places with a purpose in mind.

Many may seem to have it all together, but they are no different than anyone else. We all go through valleys of one sort or another. The good news is that in those valleys, the Lord promises his presence. We do not have to walk the isolated valley roads alone any longer.

As you travel through life, know that you can walk with God through every valley, up to the mountains, or in the high meadows of life. As you journey through the valleys of life, be encouraged by the footprints of God's mightiest sons and daughters that lie before you. The King of kings walked with them, and he will likewise be beside you on your journey. You are in good company.

- God is drawing you to himself. Open your heart and give your concerns to him.
- What are some of God's promises to his children? Write a few of them down and carry them with you over the next few days. Be encouraged! God loves you.
- Seek to encourage someone on his or her journey. Point the people in your life to our God who never leaves nor forsakes.

THE KING'S TABLE

As for Mephibosheth, said the king,
he shall eat at my table, as one of the king's sons.
2 Samuel 9:11

READ 2 SAMUEL 9:1–13.

THERE ARE MANY stories of love and compassion in the Bible, but one has always been special to me. It is the fulfillment of a promise to a dear friend. King David had come to reign over Israel. Saul, the old king, was dead. Sadly, so was his son, who happened to be David's best friend. Before Jonathan died, he made David swear that when he became king, he would deal kindly with his children. That was not the custom of the day, because any children or grandchildren of the previous king could assert themselves as the true king and cause rebellion (1 Samuel 20).

At first, it seemed that none of Jonathan's children survived. That all changed one day when someone discovered a son of Jonathan who had survived. The child had been hidden in fear for his life. His name was Mephibosheth, and he had been lame from the age of five through no fault of his own. His nurse fled in haste after hearing the fate of Jonathan and Saul—the boy's father and grandfather. In her panic, the child was injured. Since that time, he had been hopeless and helpless. It seemed as though he was condemned to live a poor and bleak existence.

When David heard that one of Jonathan's sons lived, he immediately sent his servant to bring Mephibosheth to his palace. His promise to Jonathan was unwavering, and in turn, his promise to the poor young Mephibosheth was that every need he had would be met by the provision of the king.

How many Mephibosheths do we encounter in our daily lives? Many people have been let down in their childhoods or as young people. They are spiritually injured, unable to help themselves. We were all once in need just as Mephibosheth was in need. We needed the loving hand of the King to reach down to us, lift us up, and bring us to the table of God's grace. Like Mephibosheth, we are now treated as sons and daughters of the King. Many seem content to dine on the leftovers of the world, but as children of the King, we have a continual feast before us. Why should we settle for this worlds scraps?

What a joy to be in the presence of the King! May we realize what a feast there is in the Word of God. May we drink and be refreshed by the cup of his Spirit and be strengthened for the journey ahead. May we carry the message to a broken world, so others too may eat from the King's table continually.

- Are you eating at the table of this world? Its food will never satisfy; it will only leave you hungrier. Instead, sit at the table with the King of kings today and fellowship with him.
- To sit at the King's table is a privilege. We do not deserve it. How should that truth cause us respond to God?
- Spend time in the presence of the Lord. Let him refresh and strengthen you as you pray and spend time in his Word.

Our Captain

And, behold, God himself is with us as our captain, and his priests with sounding trumpets to cry alarm against you. O children of Israel, fight not against the LORD God of your fathers; for you shall not prosper. But Jeroboam caused an ambush to come about behind them: so they were in front of Judah, and the ambush was behind them. And when Judah looked back, behold, the battle was in front and behind: and they cried unto the LORD, and the priests sounded with the trumpets. Then the men of Judah gave a shout: and as the men of Judah shouted, it came to pass, that God struck Jeroboam and all Israel before Abijah and Judah.
2 Chronicles 13:12–15

READ 2 CHRONICLES 13:1–20.

G OING INTO BATTLE outnumbered two to one is frightening enough, but imagine suddenly noticing that your enemy is not only in front of you, he has ambushed you from behind. In times like that, it is wise to have the one who has all authority in heaven and earth as captain of your forces. As Christians, we are engaged in a continual warfare. The enemy lays ambushes behind us in the form of disappointments, failures, and losses. He places before us his weapons of doubt, worry, and fear.

We often wait to see how the battle goes before we praise God. But the sound of the trumpets and the shout of the warriors in 2 Chronicles 13:14–15 were acts of faith. It can be discouraging to see how vastly outnumbered we are in this sin-sick world, and it is easy to forget who is actually in control. We can and should praise God in spite of what we see or feel, because he is faithful, and his love is immeasurable.

There are times in our lives when we feel overwhelmed. Struggles may come in the form of situations or relationships that seem impossible. Those days could be discouraging if there were no hope. But thankfully, there is hope, and that hope is as real as the Lord himself. The apostle Paul encourages us with these words: "Be anxious for nothing, but in every thing by prayer and supplication with thanksgiving let your requests be made known unto God. And the peace of God, which passes all understanding, shall keep your hearts and minds through Christ Jesus" (Philippians 4:6–7). Though our battles may differ, our captain is the same Lord. He has never lost a battle. He won the victory over death, hell, and the grave, and he is the same yesterday, today, and always.

Our confidence is in our captain; his name is Jesus, and he will never leave us or forsake us. Whatever battle you face today, go ahead and praise him in advance. Praise him for the victory he will bring. He is God, and there is none beside him. If he is your captain, it matters not that you are outnumbered or that the enemy is large; you are already victorious. Turn to him in faith knowing that he has already secured the victory.

- Are there areas or situations in your life that seem impossible? Spend time praying right now. Do not move on in your day without giving them to God.
- Ask the Lord to give you eyes to see and a heart to understand your situations from God's perspective. Ask him for wisdom on how to proceed.
- Rest in the Lord as you place your confidence in him, knowing that he understands where you are and is walking with you.

God Knows

*He heals the broken in heart, and binds up their
wounds.
He tells the number of the stars; he calls them all
by their names.
Great is our Lord, and of great power: his understanding is infinite.
Psalm 147:3–5*

Read Psalm 147:1–11.

I N THREE SHORT verses, we see a grand display of three of the
many attributes of our God. "His understanding is infinite"
(Psalm 147:5). He is the source of all knowledge. There is nothing
to be known that he does not know. While man is ever learning
and growing in knowledge, everything man can know has always
been known to God.

Not only does God know all, but also he understands all. We go through seasons when we don't understand why things happen the way they do, when nothing makes sense. You prayed for healing, but sickness came. You prayed for peace, yet trouble found you. You prayed for faith, but storm clouds of doubt seem to be all around you. We may not understand, but rest assured, GOD DOES! As his children, we need not understand all the particulars—only that what he is doing is for our good and his glory.

"He tells the number of the stars; he calls them all by their names" (Psalm 147:4). If God cares enough to name the stars he created, to know each and every one of them, and to call them by their names, he is most certainly keenly aware of each and every one of us. He is aware of every need, of every care, of every burden. Jesus said, "Come unto me, all you that labor and are heavy laden, and I will give you rest" (Matthew 11:28). He knows, and he cares.

"He heals the broken in heart, and binds up their wounds" (Psalm 147:3). Has your heart ever been broken? The answer, of course, is yes. Maybe a child forsook the godly upbringing you gave. Maybe a broken marriage left your heart in pieces. Maybe a friendship you thought would last a lifetime fell apart. If you are a Christian, when the Holy Spirit convicted you of your sin and you came to Christ in repentance, brokenness was the state of your heart. I remember how the realization that Jesus died on the cross for my sin broke my heart. The guilt and shame that were rightfully mine, he bore at Calvary. That is heartbreaking to the sinner. But praise God for his healing! Isaiah wrote, "With his stripes we are healed" (Isaiah 53:5). God will heal the broken in heart. He will never leave or forsake you. He welcomes you in, so no matter where you find yourself, know that he is waiting for you with open arms.

- Contemplate God's love and care for you. There is not one thing on your heart that he does not know about already. He is ready and waiting for you to come to him with your cares and concerns. Do not wait. Stop right now and bring them to him.
- How does understanding God's wondrous power encourage you to follow him today?
- If God has the power to appoint stars and name them, he also has the power to help you and others in their struggles. Do not rely on your own strength and wisdom. Yield to the Lord and ask him to guide and strengthen you.

SCARLET RED

Come now, and let us reason together, says the LORD: though your sins be as scarlet [red], they shall be as white as snow; though they are red like crimson, they shall be as wool.
Isaiah 1:18

READ ISAIAH 1:16–20.

THE SCARLET WORM, when ready to give birth, attaches herself to the trunk of a tree so firmly and permanently that she will never leave again. The eggs are deposited and protected beneath her body until the larvae hatch and grow to the point that they are able to live on their own. As the mother worm dies, she releases a crimson red fluid that stains her body and the surrounding wood. Long ago, the scarlet worms were collected to make red dyes.

As the scarlet worm is determined to die on her tree trunk so that new life might come forth, so Christ was willing to die for you and me so that we who were dead in sin may have life everlasting through faith in his death and resurrection. Jesus, so eager to do the will of the Father, was nailed to the cross. Yet it was not the Roman nails that held him there; it was his love for you and me.

Have you ever wondered why the harlot Rahab helped the spies of Israel escape through her window by a scarlet red cord? She believed in their God, and that belief led her by faith to trust the spies. Hebrews 11:31 says, "By faith the harlot Rahab perished not with them that believed not, when she had received the spies with peace." Before the spies left, they said, "Behold, when we come into the land, you shall bind this line of scarlet thread in the window which you let us down by: and you shall bring your father, and your mother, and your brothers, and all your father's household, home with you" (Joshua 2:18).

At the Passover, God told the people of Israel (who were in Egyptian bondage at the time) that the death angel would pass through the land. His instructions were clear: place the blood of a lamb on the doorpost. God said, "And when I see the blood, I will pass over you" (Exodus 12:13). The scarlet color runs through Scripture with the stories of forgiveness, redemption, and rescue.

May we boldly and thankfully display the scarlet cord of our faith to the world through the window of our soul so the world may see the evidence of Christ in us. What cause we have to rejoice!

- What does the scarlet red cord in Rahab's window and the blood on the doorpost at the Passover signify?
- Jesus willingly died for your sins. What does that say about God's love for us? How does that knowledge change your life?
- How should this truth change the way you live right now?

And when [Jesus] entered into a ship, his disciples followed him. And, behold, there arose a great storm in the sea, insomuch that the ship was covered with the waves: but he was asleep. And his disciples came to him, and awoke him, saying, Lord, save us: we are about to die. And he said unto them, Why are you fearful, O you of little faith? Then he arose, and rebuked the winds and the sea; and there was a great calm. But the men marveled, saying, What manner of man is this, that even the winds and the sea obey him!
Matthew 8:23–27

READ ISAIAH 41:10.

A storm came through last night. The National Weather Service predicted it was coming. I looked at the radar to see the image and direction of this storm and went peacefully to bed. As I drifted off to sleep, I could hear the rumbling thunder getting closer, but all was well. It would continue to be so, because the hand that directed the lightning and thunder was the same hand that brushed my brow as I drifted off to sleep. As the bright sun rose over the mountain, it was easy to see the storm had passed. All was well.

Some will consider all to be well only in the absence of all troubles and trials. But others somehow have the ability to say that all is well in the midst of those hard times. What's the difference? The answer lies in who is at the helm of your ship. When we follow Jesus, we can rest assured that all will be well.

Some of the disciples were fishermen by trade. Certainly, they were no strangers to storms upon the sea. But the storm in Matthew 8 must have been different. It must have been one at which even the best shipmasters would tremble. But remember, "His disciples followed him" (Matthew 8:23), and it made all the difference. Jesus was with them in the midst of the storm.

There will inevitably be storms in all our lives. Will Jesus be with you when they hit? If you are a believer, then you need not worry. The answer is yes! You do not have to ride out any storm in your power or by yourself. Follow him, and he will lead you through. But maybe you are not a true follower of Jesus. Could it be that you are sailing across the water alone, and Jesus is not present? There is good news: you can turn to him in faith at this very moment. He will hear you and come to you, bringing his salvation with him.

Be encouraged. God says, "Fear not; for I am with you: be not dismayed; for I am your God: I will strengthen you; yes, I will help you; yes, I will uphold you with the right hand of my righteousness" (Isaiah 41:10). May the strength and peace of God fill your heart today.

- Have you ever gone through a difficult time in your life? If so, how did you feel during those times?
- What does it look like to go through a difficult time while you are walking closely with Jesus? What would it look like to go through those times without him?
- Whether you are in the midst of a storm or not, memorize Isaiah 41:10. God will use his Word in your life and to encourage others.

NOT ALONE

But [Elijah] went a day's journey into the wilder-
ness, and came and sat down under a juniper tree:
and he asked that he might die; and said, It is
enough; now, O LORD, take away my life; for I
am not better than my fathers.
1 Kings 19:4

READ 1 KINGS 19:1-7.

H OW COULD A great prophet like Elijah find himself in such
a miserable state and ready to die? Where was his faith? He
was still the servant of God—the same God who had used ravens
to feed him bread and meat in the morning and the evening at
the brook called Cherith. The same God fed him by the hand of
the widow at Zarephath and caused the grain barrel and the oil
to never run dry. He was the same God who, at Elijah's prayer,

had rained down fire from heaven, consuming the water-soaked sacrifice on Mount Carmel to give him victory over four hundred prophets of Baal.

What reason could the prophet possibly have to be so depressed as to ask God to take his life? Had he forgotten the delivering power of God? We read this account and wonder: what reason could this great man of God have for being so pitiful?

As Christians, we read the Bible, go to church, and hear the Word of God taught and preached. We have seen God work time and time again. We know his awesome power and provision, we testify to answered prayer, and we rejoice in his promises, knowing that he is faithful. Even with all this, sometimes we find ourselves on what seems to be a journey into the desert. We feel alone, even in a crowd, wondering, "God, where are you?" When we hear others talk of faith, we feel dejected, because we feel spiritually weak.

Well not to worry. Being on a journey in the wilderness may not be as bad as it seems. After all, God sent his angel to be Elijah's personal chef. And on the strength of that meal, Elijah was able to journey for forty days. Sure, Elijah complained to God about his situation. Israel had forsaken God's covenant, torn down the altars, and killed the godly prophets so that he felt like the only one left. I think we can all feel this way at times. But how we feel does not always indicate what is true. God reassured Elijah that there were another seven thousand men in Israel who had not bowed their knee to the false gods. Elijah felt like he was the only one, but there were others.

Be of good cheer! You are not alone, even on a desert journey. And while the desert is not a place you want to stay, it can be a place of revival and renewed strength.

- Why is it so comforting and exciting that God knows where you are at this moment and desires to walk with you? Turn to him and give thanks for his goodness.
- Think of all the ways God has been faithful to you and write them down.
- Do you know someone who is in need of encouragement? Some of the greatest joy you will ever receive is when you seek to encourage others. Make a list of people in need of encouragement and seek to reach out to them this week.

THE POTTER'S WORK

Then I went down to the potter's house, and,
behold, he was working on the wheels.
Jeremiah 18:3

READ JEREMIAH 18:1–4.

THE POTTER WORKING is a beautiful illustration of the Lord's work in the life of the believer. First, notice how the Lord called Jeremiah to "go down" to the potter's house in verse 2. To understand the working of the potter, one must first "go down." Likewise, before there can be honor, there must first be humility (Proverbs 15:33). The apostle Peter said, "Humble yourselves therefore under the mighty hand of God, that he may exalt you in due time" (1 Peter 5:6).

After going down to the potter's house, Jeremiah was ready to hear the Word of the Lord. Once he heard, God also wanted him to see. And what he saw was a vessel of clay that had been damaged in the hand of the potter. Being the vessels of clay that we are, we are also damaged by sin. For us to become vessels of honor, it is necessary that we be made new. Notice the potter doesn't merely patch up the old vessel; he breaks down the clay and makes it another vessel. Jesus said to Nicodemus, "You must be born again" or made over (John 3:7). We are not a new version of our former self; we are new creatures. The apostle Paul stated it this way: "Therefore if any man be in Christ, he is a new creature" (2 Corinthians 5:17).

How glorious to place our lives in the hands of the great potter of the universe and have him mold and shape us into vessels of honor. Once molded, shaped, and cured, a vessel is ready for glazing. Glazing has a two-fold purpose. It first seals the vessel to keep its contents secure so that nothing inside leaks out and nothing outside gets in. This process is much like the working of the Holy Spirit in the life of the believer.

One last thing happens before the glaze is fired in the kiln: the potter etches his signature on the vessel. Many potters place this on the bottom of the piece to identify the vessel as belonging to the potter. When you entered into a personal relationship with Christ, not only did he write his name upon your heart, but he also wrote your name in heaven.

After the glaze is applied, the clay is ready for the kiln. The fire of the kiln bakes the glaze into the vessel. This part of the process is the part that most of us would rather avoid. As Christians, we are destined to some degree of suffering in the fires of affliction.

Beloved, think it not strange concerning the fiery trial which is to try you, as though some strange thing happened unto you: But rejoice, inasmuch as you are partakers of Christ's sufferings; that, when his glory shall be revealed, you may be glad also with exceeding joy.

—1 PETER 4:12-13

While there are many characteristics that help us identify the master potter's work (such as love, joy, peace, longsuffering, gentleness, goodness, meekness, faith, and temperance), the one sure way to know the maker of the life and the potter of the Christian vessel is when a life is turned upside down. When everything that can go wrong does, when nothing makes any sense, when everything that should be up is down and everything that should be down is up, then you can see the signature of the potter.

Every vessel in the potter's house is valuable. We serve different purposes, but all are of immense value. When things get tough, keep in mind, this potter only makes noble and exalted vessels.

- Why is it comforting to know that God is molding and shaping you?
- For what purpose is he doing this work in your life?
- What would it look like to humbly live as one of God's noble and exalted vessels?

FLOURISHING PALMS

The righteous shall flourish like the palm tree: he shall grow like a cedar in Lebanon. Those that be planted in the house of the LORD shall flourish in the courts of our God.
Psalm 92:12–13

READ PSALM 92.

THE LORD IS our God, and he keeps his word. He is faithful to every promise he ever made. Dear believer, stop for a moment and consider this short passage of Scripture. I know you are busy. You might be at work or getting ready for your job. You may even be running late for something, but stop for a brief moment and refresh your thirsty soul. Stop for a moment, sip from the fountain of God's Word. Be refreshed by yet another cup of his promises. Having been made righteous through the blood of Christ, you are guaranteed to flourish.

The palm tree is a very different type of tree. Unlike most trees, it doesn't branch out. It grows straight and tall. It has large leaves and produces fruit. It provides shelter from the heat and food for the weary traveler. Like other trees, however, the palm receives its life-sustaining nourishment and necessary water from its roots. After the children of Israel crossed the Red Sea, they came to a place called Elim, where there were twelve wells of water and seventy palm trees (Exodus 15:27). They camped by the waters. It was an oasis! Elim means "place of rest."

As believers, we receive our sustenance from sources unseen, just as the palm receives nourishment through it roots. Our sustenance comes from time in prayer, time in the Word, and fellowship with our Savior. The church is the spiritual oasis, and as a believer, you are a valuable member of that palm grove. The church is to be a place for the world to find rest and drink the sweet waters of God's truth.

Another unique quality of the palm is its ability to withstand storms. Regardless of how strong the wind, the palm will bend and bow, but it rarely breaks. Is not that like the Christian character? In the midst of life's storms, we may bend because of the wind, but we ultimately find strength to ride out the storm because we have been strengthened and sustained by the Lord. After each storm, we find our spiritual roots reaching a little deeper, and our life is a little stronger. We are prepared for the next wind that may come.

It is rare to see a lone palm tree, because they typically grow in groves like those of Elim. There is strength in numbers. One palm helps break the storm wind for the others, and together they survive the worst of storms. Galatians 6:2 tells us to bear on another's burdens, and Hebrews 10:25 reminds us to not forsake coming together with other believers. We were created for community and are stronger when we are a part of one. So let us rest together in those strong promises as God intended for us to.

- Take time to be refreshed in prayer. Spend time in God's Word and talking with him.
- Are you in a Sunday school class or a small group where you can get to know and encourage others as you are known and encouraged yourself? If not, ask God to help you find a group with whom to connect.
- Is your life a shelter for those who do not know Jesus? Are you living and speaking in such a way that the spiritually thirsty know they can come to you for answers?

SPIRITUAL DNA

Therefore if any man is in Christ, he is a new creature:
old things are passed away; behold, all things are become new.
2 Corinthians 5:17

READ 2 CORINTHIANS 5:17–21.

WHEN WE ARE born again, we begin new lives. We are new creatures in Christ. Although new creatures, we are not yet completely conformed to the image of Christ. Much like a newborn baby, we will possess certain similarities of our fathers. But as we grow and mature, we may begin to look and act more and more like them. Those of us who have a great love and admiration for our natural fathers begin to mimic them. We walk as they walk and talk like they talk. We want to be like them. And guess what? If you didn't have a great earthly father, you can have the Father of all fathers who loves at all times and never leaves nor forsakes. All of us need that Father. The same is true for the inner man. There is an inborn desire to be like our heavenly Father. It is in our spiritual DNA.

We struggle with the desires of the flesh. The struggle between our natural flesh and the Spirit of God within us is a battle. It is why the apostle Paul said of his life, "When I would do good, evil is present with me" (Romans 7:21). But God's love for his children is so powerful that he will transform us into the image of his son.

Often, he will allow circumstances in our lives to work as a purifying fire. When it seems we are in the furnace of affliction, dear believer, realize that God is using these seemingly unwanted and unwelcomed situations to burn away the impurities in our lives, much like the silversmith purifies his silver in the furnace. Only when he can see his reflection in the silver does he know he has finished the work.

So be of good cheer, child, and know that—if you are in one of those furnaces at this time in your life—it is truly for your good and God's glory. May we finish strong!

- Why is it comforting to know that God is working in you during difficult days?
- Do you have a desire to follow God? If so, where is your flesh always trying to lead you?
- If you do not have a desire to follow the Lord, turn to him in faith now and ask him to change you.

*This devotion was written the day after Reverend Hood was diagnosed with ALS.

TRUE RICHES

---

*There is one who makes himself rich, yet has
nothing:
There is one who makes himself poor, yet has great
riches.*
Proverbs 13:7

READ ECCLESIASTES 2.

MANY DEVASTATED LIVES lay along the road to fame and riches. The appetite for material wealth has left a multitude malnourished and starving. Though for some such a pursuit may have started out as virtuous ambition, soon it becomes an insatiable appetite fueled by greed, pride, and self-interest. It is sad to see those with material wealth so spiritually poor, but all of us can find ourselves in this place if we seek wealth as our hope and fulfillment.

Solomon, a great man of wealth, knew this all too well. He said, "I made great works for myself; I built houses for myself; I planted vineyards for myself: I made gardens and orchards for myself, and I planted trees in them of all kind of fruits: I made pools of water for myself, with which to water the wood that brings forth trees: I got servants and maidens for myself, and had servants born in my house; also I had great possessions of great and small cattle above all that were in Jerusalem before me" (Ecclesiastes 2:4–7). He had it all. Yet something was missing. At the end of the building, growing, and acquiring, Solomon came to this conclusion: "Behold, all was in vain" (Ecclesiastes 2:11).

Jesus told the parable of a rich man whose ground brought forth bounty. In three verses, Luke 12:17–19, this man used the terms "I," "me," and "my" 11 times. In the end, God said, "You fool, this night your soul shall be required of you: then who shall those things be, which you have stored up?" (Luke 12:20)

Be not deceived, however; material riches are not the only wealth that separates people's hearts from God. Those who do not have a coin to their names can still make themselves rich with pride and love of sin and so find themselves in the same perilous waters. There lies within the heart of each of us a longing, a hunger, a desire for peace, joy, and fulfillment that can never be satisfied by anything this world has to offer. Such peace can only be experienced through a personal relationship with our Creator, our God, through the Lord Jesus Christ.

So who are the poor who truly have great riches in Proverbs 13:7? These are the ones who have humbled themselves and surrendered their lives to Christ. These are the ones who have true riches that do not fade away and that cannot be taken. Jesus said, "Lay up for yourselves treasures in heaven, where neither moth nor rust corrupt, and where thieves do not break in nor steal" (Matthew 6:20). These are the ones who understand that you gain by giving in the kingdom of God. Jesus said, "For whosoever will save his life shall lose it: but whosoever will lose his life for my sake, the same shall save it. For what is a man advantaged, if he gain the whole world, and lose himself, or be cast away?" (Luke 9:24–25).

Would you like to be truly wealthy? Then make yourself poor by shedding your pride, your love for the acceptance of this world. Turn from sin and humble yourself before God, and you too can have great riches.

- What are some things in which you have placed too much value?
- Do the things of this world give you peace in the depths of your soul?
- Humble yourself before God. Seek the riches of his presence. You will be led to a place of thankfulness where you can really enjoy the blessings of life.

HOME

Let not your heart be troubled: you believe in God,
believe also in me.
In my Father's house are many mansions:
If it were not so, I would have told you.
I go to prepare a place for you.
John 14:1–3

READ JOHN 14:1–7.

EAVEN IS A place. It is not a feeling, a state of mind, or a dream, but an actual place. It is a prepared place for a prepared people. Why would God send his only son to a sin-sick, hate-filled world that did not—and still does not—want him? Why would Jesus willingly suffer an agonizing death on a cruel Roman cross and then go to prepare a place so beautiful and glorious that the human imagination cannot comprehend it? Of course, the answer is love.

We know that in heaven there will be no more sin, sorrow, pain, or tears. John says in Revelation 21:4, "And God shall wipe away all tears from their eyes; and there shall be no more death, neither sorrow, nor crying, neither shall there be any more pain: for the former things are passed away." The Apostle Peter wrote, "Blessed be the God and Father of our Lord Jesus Christ, which according to his abundant mercy has given us a new birth into a lively hope by the resurrection of Jesus Christ from the dead, To an inheritance incorruptible, and undefiled, and that fades not away, reserved in heaven for you" (1 Peter 1:3–4). Reserved IN HEAVEN FOR YOU! How marvelous it is to trust in the finished work of Jesus on the cross. See his work in the life of believers here in this world and know that when our journey here is complete, he has prepared for us a place in glory where we shall praise him throughout the endless ages. There will be no need for preaching or praying, only endless praise to the Lamb of God.

Heaven is a place prepared for a people prepared. Are you prepared?

- Our sin has separated us from a relationship with God. Jesus came and paid the penalty for our sin and now offers his forgiveness and the restoration of our relationship with the Father. Do you have that forgiveness and relationship Jesus is offering?
- If you have not yet trusted Christ for forgiveness from sin, believe in the Lord and open your heart to receive his gift of forgiveness and freedom.
- To turn away and say no to God is to reject the love of a Father. Let nothing stand in your way at this moment. If you have been forgiven and know the Lord, there are still times that you might not be walking with him. Turn back in repentance to God and his love.

PEACE THAT MAKES A DIFFERENCE

And the fruit of righteousness is sown in peace by
them that make peace.
James 3:18

READ JOHN 14:23-27.

I F WE VIEW the events of the day from the perspective of the world, we would say that they are troubling, to say the least. There seems to be conflict on almost every continent. Many cultures seem to be in moral free fall. Leaders appear to be unable to distinguish the truth from a lie, and some just do not care about the difference. Some will say the world is simply suffering from issues of misunderstanding. If nations, communities, or individuals could somehow understand each other, we could all get along and coexist. Others say it's a problem of education. If we could only teach those who seek to harm us that we are peace-loving people who mean them no harm, they would respond with peace. Then we could all sit around the campfire of peace and be as one.

Jesus said in John 14:27, "Peace I leave with you, my peace I give unto you: not as the world gives, give I unto you. Let not your heart be troubled, neither let it be afraid." But we can never have the peace of God if we refuse to make peace with God. The only way to have peace with God is through his son, Jesus Christ. When we raise the white flag of surrender and lay down our weapons of pride and self-will, we not only receive the peace of God, but we can then begin to sow the seeds that will bring forth the fruit of righteousness in our lives and the lives of those around us.

This world might be a mess, but if you read your Bible, you should not be discouraged. You and I are here now for a reason. God has us here, at this time, to serve his purpose. As the recipients of God's peace through his son, Jesus Christ, let us sow the fruit of righteousness in peace, with the full knowledge that we will reap what we sow. "And let us not be weary in doing good: for in due season we shall reap, if we do not give up" (Galatians 6:9).

He that goes forth weeping, bearing precious seed for sowing, shall doubtless come again with rejoicing, bringing his sheaves with him.

—Psalm 126:6

You are making a difference. Keep sowing; there is a harvest coming!

- Are you experiencing the peace of God? Remember, you can never have the peace of God if you refuse to make peace with God. Spend time opening your heart to the Lord and allowing him to show you anything that stands in the way of your relationship with him.
- Ask God to give you the strength to walk in obedience today and to sow seeds of righteousness in your life and relationships.
- Is there anyone with whom you do not have peace? If at all possible, live at peace with everyone. (Romans 12:18) Do not let your pride destroy a relationship. Ask and offer forgiveness today.

THE BEST FOR LAST

And I saw a new heaven and a new earth:
for the first heaven and the first earth were passed
away;
and there was no more sea.
Revelation 21:1

READ REVELATION 21:1-8.

S OMETIMES WE GET so entangled in the day-to-day issues of this life that we lose sight of the big picture. As King Solomon put it, we allow "the little foxes" to spoil the sweet grape vines of joy and peace (Song of Solomon 2:15). We allow the enemy to make himself at home in our minds and hearts, and he devours the sweet fruits that were sent to us as evidence of what awaits the people of God in the Promised Land the Lord has prepared for us (Numbers 13:23-24). We would be much better witnesses if we lived from day to day in confidence, knowing that God will make all things right in the end. We don't even have to worry about the wrongs that are done to us today.

The life of Job is an example of the blessings of God being greater at the end than the beginning. God did not love Job more than he loves you. Job didn't understand the what, when, why, or how of his tribulations, yet he was able to say, "Though he slay me, yet will I trust in him" (Job 13:15).

Your world may be upside down and inside out at times. It may be that nothing seems to be working out as you planned. It would serve us well to bear in mind that our plans may not be God's plan. Regardless of what you are dealing with, remember that God is saving the best for last. We need only to look at God's creative work to see evidence of this. When God created light, the Bible says, "The evening and the morning were the first day" (Genesis 1:5). We assume that every day starts out with a morning. Not so! The first day began in the evening. The hope of a new morning comes after the first evening.

We who await the return of our Lord look forward to an eternal morning where there is no night. It will be a day without end, "and there shall be no more death, neither sorrow, nor crying, neither shall there be any more pain: for the former things are passed away" (Revelation 21:4). God saves the best for last.

As beautiful as all God's creation is, we haven't seen anything yet. We can only imagine the glory that will be revealed in us and to us when Christ comes for his own and creates a new heaven and a new earth. Paul wrote that when our earthly bodies are destroyed, we will have new bodies, eternal in the heavens, not made with hands (2 Corinthians 5:1). He went on to write, "So also is the resurrection of the dead. It is sown in corruption; it is raised in incorruption: It is sown in dishonor; it is raised in glory: it is sown in weakness; it is raised in power: It is sown a natural body; it is raised a spiritual body" (1 Corinthians 15:42-44).

As good or bad as you may perceive things to be now, keep in mind, dear believer, that God is saving the best for last. What a grand finale we can expect—one that will mark an even more magnificent beginning, a beginning that will never end.

- Where is the most beautiful place you have ever seen on this earth? Remember and contemplate the specific attributes that amazed you. Consider for a moment that such places are mere shadows of what is to come.
- Now reflect on the beauty of heaven. Also take time to contemplate what it will look like to be in a perfect relationship with the Lord and other people.
- Spend time praising God for the best that is yet to come. Pray for others, and share with them God's love as you seek to go and make disciples.